THE INVITATION TO

The Invitation to the Garden

a mystical journey in five paradoxes

❧

JOANNA TULLOCH

2018

Matador
9 Priory Business Park,
Wistow Road, Kibworth Beauchamp,
Leicestershire: LE8 0RX
Tel: 0116 279 2299
Email: books@troubador.co.uk
Web: www.troubador.co.uk/matador
Twitter: @matadorbooks

ISBN 978 1789014 143

British Library Cataloguing in Publication Data.
A catalogue record for this book is available from the British Library.

Printed and bound by CPI Group (UK) Ltd, Croydon, CR0 4YY

Matador is an imprint of Troubador Publishing Ltd

PREFACE

This book tells the story of my spiritual journey and what I have learnt from it about the unconditional love that is offered to us all, whatever the problems we have to face in life. It could be seen as a modern *Pilgrim's Progress* designed especially for anyone who is struggling in the Slough of Despond. It has taken me twenty-five years to complete, but in a sense it covers my whole life with its flashbacks to childhood experiences. It is set out as a series of paradoxes, each of which leads to a learning experience: accepting the invitation (and myself), starting to see and hear what God wanted me to understand, suffering and growing through it, daring to trust, and finally coming to terms with my illness and travelling on. Much of the story is told in verse, with some Bible verses and prose flashbacks (in italics) interspersed with this.

In my teens I had anorexia nervosa, and after several unsuccessful admissions to hospital in London I was sent to a clinic near Paris; I was just turning fourteen. Although this was a terrifying experience, especially at the beginning, it did succeed in that I was able to return to school after several months, and the illness only recurred at times of particular stress such as my finals. However, I then developed severe recurrent depression, which has led to eight more hospital admissions and a lifetime of outpatient treatment. Throughout this time I have struggled to make sense of my faith, and have been given moments of insight that were like an invitation from a gentle gardener to step out of the jungle of life into the garden of his love.

I have been a Methodist local preacher for more than thirty years, and my most difficult period of illness in the 1990s coincided with my first full decade as a preacher. The invitation itself first came to me at the beginning of this decade of illness. I believe that the testimony I have to give in this book is more powerful than anything I have been able to say from the pulpit, and hope that it will reach the people who could most benefit from it.

My special thanks go to the Reverend Bob Whorton for his encouragement to finish writing *The Invitation to the Garden* and to make it public. I would also like to thank those who have read and commented on the draft text, including John and Freda Cammack, Gilli Hanna, David and Clare Matthews, Dr Stephen Merson, Mary Ronaldson, Paul and Wendy Spray, and Hannah Stammers, and to all the helpful and friendly staff at Matador. Most of all I am grateful to my husband George Tulloch for his constant love and support, and especially for copy editing, typesetting, and proofreading.

*

Several short extracts from this work were previously published as individual poems in my earlier poetry collection *A Reflection of God* (Matador, 2014).

CONTENTS

PROLOGUE

The Garden (1)

While living in the middle of the jungle,
is there not a garden we all seek,
vaguely remembered, or maybe only dreamed of:
do we not long to have it in our sight?

Can we not hear its music in our silence,
a great sad song of longing, yet of joy,
the song sung by a gentle, lonely Gardener—
do we dare to listen, touch the tree of life?

They heard the sound of the Lord God walking in the garden in the heat of the day . . . And God said to Eve, 'What is this you have done? . . . I will increase your labour and your groaning.' And He put them out of the garden.

And Jesus said to Mary Magdala, 'Why are you weeping? Who is it that you seek?' And, thinking that he was the gardener, she said, 'Tell me where you have taken him.'

And Jesus said, 'Mary.' One word. And then she knew.

The song once heard can never be forgotten,
it is the restless music of our souls.
But never say our free will has been forfeit:
we choose, all right—whether to weep or dance.

1. STARTING THE JOURNEY

Accepting

The first paradox: the way to the garden will lead you
through the jungle (*being a lesson in accepting your true nature
and that of the Gardener*)

THE TRAVELLER

It took me by surprise in every way:
a tiny church, the dark end of the day,
and only half a dozen in the pews,
straining to make their songs appear good news—
when worship is hard work for priest and flock
and eyes keep wandering off to check the clock.
Hardly an auspicious way to start
a journey to the centre of your heart.
And then there is the other thing as well—
Methodists don't have visions—or don't tell.

'Let us pray.
Let us confess our sins to God.'

Let us confess,
let us confess,
let us descend into that putrid mess
where all our failings tie us in a knot
and tendril-like entwine us . . .
No, let's not.

Too late.
Suddenly
I had entered
this jungle of the soul.

And it was
a real jungle,
dark,
wet,
hot,
and swampy.
I was really there,
finally transported
to the slippery
rotting
claustrophobic
pit where I belong.

Many times
this swamp
had sucked me down,
but now
trapped in the yellow muck,
dripping yet thirsty,
hopeless and dirty,
I knew the nightmare
for what it was—
my life.
Frantic struggling,
inevitable but pointless,
only stirred the mud,
pulling me
further,
further,
always further
down.
Did I not know this

from of old?
Stamping through the
undergrowth
led me to the swamp,
so why go on stamping
with feet held fast?
Why not just sink
into the muck
from which I came?

She shouted and shouted, and nobody came. She grabbed desperately at the grass on the bank, trying not to slip further down into the bog. In the dry season, would they come and find her there, still wearing her Wellingtons? When she was tired of shouting and couldn't any more, then he came. The gardener. Strong arms lifting her and carrying her back to the safety of the garden, leaving only the Wellingtons. Maybe they are there still.

So when I saw
the vision,
the hand of grace
extending through the trees,
I knew at once
that this must be
the Gardener,
I knew that He alone
could hear my cries.

It was just a hand really,
but never before
and never since
has such a hand been seen:
coming from light
it pointed to light,

transparent, yet
having substance,
real help
and real hope
to offer.
In the moment
of that courteous invitation
to step into the garden
from the mire,
in that turquoise and yellow moment
there was time and no time,
now and all time.
And, oh,
there was mercy,
and grace to believe in mercy,
grace to be accepted
and be loved.
Can I recreate
the silence—
it was
speaking
but no words,
music
but no tune,
silence fit to heal a thousand wounds.
And it was invitation:
'Come,
this is all for you,
please be my guest.
Without you
there cannot be a garden.

Come, if you will—
but only if you will—
to make my garden complete.'

So that was it really,
a hand between the trees,
an invitation,
the invitation to the garden.
And the knowledge
that if
there was anything,
anything at all
I must say 'Yes' to
in my life,
it was this:
this gentle,
this courteous,
this quiet
invitation,
this hand
that I saw
in a dreary church,
in a dripping jungle,
this hand
holding out
life.

You don't forget experiences like these
and as the hand withdrew behind the trees
I vowed to seek that garden all my days
no matter what the cost; in many ways

I hardly knew what that could mean for me
and that might be as well, as I would see.

It only takes
one word
to accept—
but this
goes over words
and through words
and past words,
this takes
a thousand or more
wordsworths
of the soul.

In order to accept
His invitation
I found I had to *be*
the invited one,
to allow Him
to choose *me*,
mucky and hopeless
in the mire,
to declare *me*
acceptable,
beautiful,
needed in His garden.
This was hard,
is hard;
and the harder
I tried
the more mud

stuck to me,
the more I stank,
and I knew it.

The lesson of the swamp is learned in stages,
the jungle and the mire are always there;
and I had thought to go straight to the garden
while feeling still the pit was more my fare.

Gardener! Gardener! Help!
I am still in the swamp
and I am sinking!
Why do I search
and never find the entrance?
Why do I always
get in such a mess?

THE GARDENER

Be still, my child, and do not fret.
Be still, and stop your frantic struggling.
You only need to seek me in your heart,
incline the ear of your heart,
open the eyes of your heart,
and you will know me with you once again.

Turn to me,
gaze on me
and see how much I love you.
Do you think I'd ever give you up?

Turn to me,
gaze on me,

try to turn away from all your failings.
Don't you think I know you through and through?

Turn to me,
gaze on me,
leave me to decide how best to show you
that you
and your mess
and your struggles
are for me to gaze on.

You can look at me and find great beauty:
when I gaze on you I find the same.

You cannot accept the gift I offer
while you are expecting to be pure;
you must first accept your own true nature,
love, as I do, your humanity.

Remember how it was when you were tiny,
how you loved to spend time in the woods.
There was excitement there, and there was danger—
when you played there you could truly live.

Sometimes, yes, the danger sucked you downwards
and you were forced to shout aloud for help,
but then there were the strong arms of the gardener,
the shoulder-ride, the garden that was home.

I want you now to live as you could then,
running free and happy to take risks;
I know you need the thrills and the excitement
that living in the jungle brings to you.

Remember that I made you and I know you:
if I choose to rejoice and not condemn,
who are you to try to escape the jungle?
Who are you to say my love is wrong?

Though you're mucky, I will always love you.
Though you fail, I want you to be mine.
If you'll only turn to me for pardon
we'll rejoice in you and make you whole.

Accept, then, that you want and need the jungle;
accept your own true nature as I do.
This time I can't bring you to the garden,
but I'll always guide you and forgive.

Accept from me the courage for your journey,
accept what you could never give yourself:
the knowledge that you are uniquely precious,
a plant of beauty and of immense worth.

My garden cannot be complete without you,
and so I pray that you will journey on,
consent to be imperfect and yet precious,
consent to weep, and dance, and hurt, and grow.

Only remember that amazing moment,
the point of invitation and of joy,
and, in the darkness, it shall be a beacon
and, in the jungle, it shall clear the sky.

Be still, my child. Do not fret. I am with you, always.

2. FINDING THE PATH

Seeing and hearing

The second paradox: be you ever so clever, you will never find your
way with your intellect (*being a lesson in seeing with the heart and
treasuring glimpses of glory*)

THE TRAVELLER

Two years passed, and life went hurtling on,
its busyness more frantic as its pain increased;
I worked with words and thought and cerebral pursuits
and on my day of rest I preached more words.

And yet the truth I found was not complete:
words could not reach that aching void within
that screamed my need of God, not in the brain
but deep in the raw unanswered place of pain.

Simple silence was the balm for this
and as I sought to apply it more and more
it proved the sweetest ointment
for a soul distressed.

So it was I found myself one night
sitting looking at an abbey ruin
at Glastonbury, where I was on retreat,
but trying to sneak in some working time.

In this great place of silence I still tried
to work out my salvation with my mind—
time for another lesson, a new step,
a vision, if you like, a flash of light.

The curtains were open and the lonely ruin
Stood black and majestic to an azure sky.
Blue, royal, ultramarine,
azure, navy, cerulean, teal.
The words of the thesaurus filled my mind.

'I haven't got enough brain in my head, I haven't got enough brain in my head.' She said it over and over to herself as she grappled with the exam questions. She had to win the scholarship or her parents couldn't afford to send her to this school . . . But she didn't, and they did. Now she had to do well to repay them . . .

'I haven't got enough brain in my head, I haven't got enough brain in my head.' She repeated it as she waited for the class exam results to go up on the board. Oh dear, no! A hundred per cent. Perfection. Now nothing less could ever be good enough. They would always expect perfection, always want her to jump the next hurdle . . .

'I haven't got enough brain in my head, I haven't got enough brain in my head.' She recited it to herself as she tried to revise for the summer exams, out in the school garden. But a little green aphid on her book had other ideas. It danced for her on the page and she noticed how perfect it was, how much more important it was than brain-work. This kind of perfection was so much more beautiful and wholesome than the hurdles . . .

Something stirred inside her and it wasn't in her mind. She felt full to bursting point somewhere around her middle. The little aphid had taught her a new emotion: joy.

What made me look up?
I still don't know.
This time not an aphid,
that's for sure.
A flash, a flicker
in a distant tree,

a sky that offered meaning
for the senseless words?
Maybe a sudden silence
that was more than hush,
a hint of balm
and vision,
glory breaking into peace.

Anyway,
it started in a tree.
Was it the one
I had seen
split to its roots,
standing in two parts
yet somehow in leaf?
Or was it perhaps
the fabled thorn,
sprouted in mystery,
famed for its Christmas flowers?

Maybe it was neither,
but a tree out there,
deep in the abbey garden,
sprung to light;
myriad candle flames
twinkled
on its branches,
winking at my dullness,
daring me to look.
'No, this is too corny—
not a burning bush?'
My clever mind,

stupid as ever,
challenged my eyes.
Yet even my brain
knew
this was something special,
even my intellect
couldn't scorn true light.

And so I peered,
dodging my reflection
in the glass.
This was something more
than meets the eye,
more than a tree,
more than light.

And as I peered
and dodged
and wondered,
something else appeared—
a lovely girl,
her face suffused with light,
in azure robes
melting
with the sky.

She was looking—
just looking—
at the tree,
floating almost
in the sky above.
She was serene
yet urgent,

wanting me to see;
peace and promise,
loveliness and light.

'Look—
just look—'
she seemed to say,
'see with your heart
the garden
that is here.
You will only glimpse it
as you travel on,
but hold it
in your soul
to nourish
and sustain.
Remember the glory,
like a blinding flash:
is this not more lovely
than all worldly gifts?
Mind well the invitation
to the garden-life:
your true self
is the only one
can find the way.
And finding your true self
will lead you far,
deep into darkness,
to a silent world
where you will hear the secrets
of a hidden life.
Your intellect is precious,

but for worldly gifts:
don't let it talk you out of
heavenly things.

Grasp hold of glory
as it flashes by,
give it to your soul,
a balm for darkness there.
Learn to use your heart
to see and hear,
and even your bleak path
will shine with cheer.'

Then, even as she spoke, she faded in the sky,
the tree returned to normal and I sat there, stunned.
Serenity herself had given time for me,
to draw me from my busyness to clarity.

Had I been seeing things? well yes, indeed!
But they had an obvious reality.
This was a sign of truth, a mystic sight
that we can only touch on fleetingly.

I'd like to say my eyes were opened then,
for everything around became so, so intense:
beauty that hurt my eyes and sounds my ears,
experience so deep it often led to tears.

But this was the time depression gripped my soul,
my darkened mind claimed notice and respect,
and, though I held these moments to my heart,
people thought me mad for what I claimed I'd seen.

A field was my reminder of the young girl's smile,
an ordinary field in which I walked my soul.
While others walked their dogs I sought the silence there
and found a peace and brightness in the early morn.

Many hours of tramping brought me to a day
when dew lay on the grass and all the snails were out,
hundreds if not thousands everywhere you looked,
gracing umbelliferae and hay and grass.

It was my moment of the 'bright field',
my latter-day aphid joy,
but this time in the tiny snails.

All sizes
were there,
large and small
and pinhead-sized.

Have you ever seen
a dewdrop and a snail
become a jewel before you,
robed in glorious light?

I could have looked
and gone my way,
I could have looked
and forgotten it.
But these tiny,
perfect creatures
seemed to speak
to me.
I had looked,
and peered, and searched

all to find an answer
in my brain.
Now,
intellect forgotten,
I just knelt in awe.
'Remember,
remember us,
the tiny snails.
The Gardener
has loved us, so,
just think now,
"How much more . . .?"'

Gardener! Thank You
for reminding me—
the garden is right here
if I will use my eyes.
I look and look
and try to use my head,
but You can touch my heart
and then, at last, I see.

THE GARDENER

Be still, my child, and do not fret.
Be still, and stop your frantic searching.
You only need to seek me in your heart,
incline the ear of your heart,
open the eyes of your heart,
and you will know me with you once again.

Turn to me,
gaze on me,

and focus on great beauty:
now you'll see I love you so much more.

Turn to me,
gaze on me,
try to turn away from all your searching:
now you'll see the garden brings you joy.

Turn to me,
gaze on me,
leave me to decide how best to show you
that you,
your depression,
all your mind's pain
are for me to gaze on.

You can look at me and find great beauty—
when I gaze on you I find the same.

I have given you great gifts to offer,
but they are not all found in your head.
If you want to serve me in my garden
you will need your heart and soul as well.

Beauty is the genius of my garden,
nature is the language of my hands;
bring the two together in your seeing,
plant the seeds of joy within your soul.

I have made you perfect in perception,
sculpted to reflect the light of joy;
you can now let light pass through the prism
without hindrance from your thoughts and fears.

Do not think, just look and feel and listen,
let the earth pass softly through your hands,
give your feet the chance to drink the dewdrops,
give your head the chance to feel the wind.

Then you'll know my real invitation
isn't about doing or the brain
but about yourself as a whole person,
intellect, but soul and body too.

I am asking nothing clever of you,
I have not a hurdle you must jump,
just a gift that you can barely spy yet:
don't be proud, just touch it as if blind.

Here's the invitation that I offer
for you to touch and treasure in the dark,
to trust it will ask nothing at all of you,
to trust it will enrich you in your search:

Relax. Drink in beauty.
It is free and necessary to you.
Be still, my child. Do not fret. I am with you, always.

INTERLUDE 1

The shadow
Psalm 63: 7

'Sing,' said the psalmist,
'Sing in the shadow of His wings.'
So I opened my mouth
and out came a plaintive keening,
not so much a melody
as a frightened howl of pain.
And I knew that my song could never be good enough,
I knew that the darkness could only get deeper,
and I bared my back and tensed me for the punishment.

'Thank you',
He said.
'Yours shall be a precious song,
born as it is from suffering and grief.
Thank you for your honesty,
for you have sung yourself.'

In place of the whip
I felt only a whisper,
the stroking of a feather,
the shadow
the shadow of His wings.

3. PLANTED IN THE DARK

Suffering and growth

The third paradox: when you reach the darkest places on your
journey and feel most alone, then the Gardener is tending you as
a plant for His garden (*being a lesson in the meaning of despair and in
recognizing true growth*)

THE TRAVELLER

I spoke before of darkness in my mind,
but what came next was blackness like the pit.
Although its shadow stalked me from my past
I couldn't then imagine half of it.

A hint was given as I walked my soul
with others on retreat in Somerset.
A place called Velvet Bottom was the spot.
Deep in a wood, a pothole caught my eye.

It was disused,
this pothole,
too dangerous
for climbers
to attempt.
Deep and dark
and shut off
by a grille,
with chains
and padlocks
keeping people
out.

Darkness,
bars,
padlocks,
FEAR.
To see it all
just made
my memory
flip.
Suddenly
I found myself
transported—
as if imprisoned
on the dark side
of the grille.
Kept in, I was,
not out,
by terror, darkness, chill.
Kept in for punishment,
for my 'own good'.
The others
were still there
in the safe wood,
could see and smell
the bluebells
and the trees.
'God be with you',
I had said to them—
and He was.
They couldn't see me,
couldn't hear my cries;
He, being with them,

seemed light years from me.
This was a nightmare echo—
I was all alone.

She shouted and shouted, but nobody came. She put her hand up in front of her face, but the darkness was so intense that she could see nothing; she had to touch her eyes to convince herself that they were still there. She had seen the nurse close and padlock the shutters, after all, and she had known then that they wouldn't admit even a chink of light from the barred windows. Perhaps in her timid cries of 'infirmière' her schoolgirl French had given her the wrong word for 'nurse' (she was later to find they were known as 'gardes' or 'keepers' anyway)? She shouted again, trying different words, but was met only with the stifling darkness and the terrifying silence which told her no one would come. They had been so nice when her parents were still there, but now they left her to her fear, her terror, a starved and frightened child in a foreign country who only wanted to die in peace. After hours of screaming, a whole night of terror, the Jekyll-and-Hyde nurse from the day before did come. But it was only for force-feeding. Then the darkness once again.

'You get what you deserve',
I had been told.
Darkness.
Terror.
Punishment.
Was this again
my lot?
To be alone,
to be afraid,
pursued
by demon-gods?
This indeed
was what I've called

the pit.
I cannot start
to tell you how it was.
But I will try
with words I wrote down
then.

First, the terror
of hospital again,
echoing with memories
of my childhood fear;
repeated and repeated
like a hammer-blow
until its every contour
filled me with despair:

'Same dead flowers
declaring dissipation;
tea bags—also dead—
decorate the room.
Shutters, locked and painted solid
block the real light.
Help! no light switch on these walls,
throwback to the dark.
Dear God, did I cross the threshold
of a past life,
coming here?
Do they speak French?
Do they dismiss one's cries?
Dead dissipation,
dead decoration,
deadening despair.

This is the pulse:
dead, dead, dead.
The hammer cruelly forces home
the nail.
Here is the epitome of pointlessness
after which any life is sane.'

Then, the demon-gods
that haunted me,
shouting in my ear
that I deserved to die,
pushing me to punishments
yet more bizarre,
goading me to cut, and burn,
and drill my flesh:

'Here I sit
on the rubbish tip
with Job,
broken glass in hand,
ready to cut the contours
of my pain
in flesh,
ready to raise the scars
and screams within
to now,
ready to die
before I'll curse my God.

'But none of this is noble.
Squalid
is what it is,
squalid and pathetic.

(I speak, of course,
for me, not Job.)

'How low can I sink?
Oh God, tell me
I won't have to take much more.

'Let me hit the bottom,
then—
believe this pile of shit
can be the mountain-top,
believe these shards
can turn into stained glass.
You alone
can raise me
from the rubbish heap,
transform,
transfigure,
turn despair to hope.'

Third, the loss of all
I thought was me:
the roles that I had
juggled hard to play—
failure as a wife, a mum, a friend,
failure in my work and preaching, too.
All that I had been
was suddenly destroyed—
what was left
but pain
and nothingness?

'Walking
down a corridor
of pain,
the walls
bowed inwards,
pressing on my head,
the floor
too slippery,
polished to a glaze,
so that I can see
my misery
reflected from my feet.
So many doors
so many doors
to open
and all without a knob,
black doors
stretching to eternity,
and when I guess
how one of them is opened
or in my frenzy
smash it with my head,
there is nothing
nothing at all
behind it—
not a view
not a world
not a thought
not a life,
and this is not peace—
it is nothingness,

nonentity,
which *is* my life now.

'Why go on?
Why open any more?
The pain says
"sink down on your knees and die".
The tiredness says the same.
But one of these doors
must open
on something,
one must lead me
somewhere sane.
Try, try to find
the door of peace—
the one door
that leads inwards
to the soul.
There are many ways out,
many doors to oblivion;
it is easy to take these.
Harder to remain
a seeker,
harder to believe
this crazy search
is its own view
its own world
its own thought
its own life,
and there is peace
wholeness
identity.

Too difficult perhaps—
but while it's there
can I end my life now?'

Most terrifying yet, my loss of God—
the silence of my prayer
was now not balm, but void.
This pit, this chasm
was worse to me than death
and so I sought to escape
into oblivion's arms:

'Waiting
always waiting
for the next moment to pass—
the ticking of the clock
that isn't here.
Waiting to do,
to talk,
to live another hour.
Waiting
interminably
for the chance to be.
Waiting
and wanting to escape.
Hell is a waiting room
and my appointment
never comes.
Oh God,
save me from myself,
or I shall self-destruct
in waiting.'

But sometimes I could pray to the true God;
it wasn't always demons and the pit.
One day as I shouted my despair,
demanding to know 'Why?', an image came.

This image,
this picture
that I saw
wasn't in the air
nor yet
before my eyes.
How can I explain it?
It was deep within,
touching
the raw place
in which
I'm really me.

Hands again.
Scarred and trembling hands,
held out to me,
cupped.
And in these hands
a cruelly broken bird.
That's all there was
at first.
No person with the hands,
no face to look at.
Just the pain,
just the brokenness
joining hands and bird.
But there was love

in this unity,
love held out to me.
Like the moment,
it was horrible
yet wonderful—
shards became
stained glass.

And then the tears.
The hands,
the bird,
were wet with them,
and I cried, too,
my tears mingling
with the rest.

Just the pain,
just the brokenness,
joining me with Christ.

Gardener! Gardener! Help!
I am hurting!
Why do I stumble
in this world of darkness?
Why is it always
punishment and pain?

THE GARDENER

Be still, my child, and do not fret.
Be still and stop your frantic screaming.
You only need to seek me with your heart,
incline the ear of your heart,

open the eyes of your heart
and you will know me with you once again.

Turn to me,
gaze on me,
and see how much I love you.
Do you think I'd send you tears and pain?

Turn to me,
gaze on me,
try to turn away from all your failings.
Do you think I'd punish and pursue?

Turn to me,
gaze on me,
leave me to decide how best to show you
that you,
your depression,
all your mind's pain
are for me to gaze on.

You can look at me and find great beauty—
when I gaze on you I find the same.

You do not get what you deserve in life:
you cannot deserve my gift of grace;
but you must accept it and receive it,
then my love can fill you from within.

'Why', you ask, 'must I endure this darkness?'
You have seen the answer in your heart,
in my hands that hold a broken creature,
in my tears that join you to the cross.

'But', you say, 'that isn't any answer,
all it does is lead me to ask more!'
Yes, that's right, for this is the way upwards,
thus the shoot grows up through the dark soil.

There is not an answer to your question
but a step to make once it is asked—
you know that you had to make your journey
all alone, to find your proper path.

You thought you were alone but I was with you,
deep within your dark heart of despair,
I was close in ways you couldn't dream of,
suffering, pruning, watering with tears.

Do not fear.
We have much in common.
And the cross is a great sign of glory.

Be still, my child. Do not fret. I am with you, always.

INTERLUDE 2

Revisiting
Psalm 63: 7 revisited

All this time my guilt
has been unquestioned;
all these years I've thought
I was to blame.
That You forgave
and loved me anyway—
yes, that was a revelation.
You stroked me with the feather
as I waited for the whip.
But now in the silence
I hear another question:
for what am I really responsible?
Now I must answer
to the me that is becoming—
no false guilt or ugliness or shame.
That You find me blameless
and even beautiful
draws me from the shadows,
helps me grasp the real.
In Your shelter
You have grown me new white feathers;
my turn now to test them,
caress with them,
risk flight.
It will not be easy
to leave self-blame behind me,
but yes, I will be-coming.
And, as I come, I sing.

4. NOWHERE TO PLACE YOUR FEET

Trusting

The fourth paradox: only when you stop looking down at your feet
will the torrent become the firm ground of the garden (*being a lesson
in accepting uncertainty and moving forward in trust*)

THE TRAVELLER

One morning I awoke in a strange place,
a hospital, but not the one I knew.
I found a consciousness all swathed in fog—
was I alive, or even really me?

I could not say how I had fetched up here,
or where I was, or what the nurses' names.
I could not make my memory work for me
or place myself in what was going on.

It was as if I sailed on some huge ship,
powerless myself but to accept what came,
propelled across a vast and misty sea
from some lost corner to a port unknown.

I struggled to regain a present self
and make some sense of what was going on.
At first I found my mind was split in two,
half recognized and spoke, the other not.

The conscious person talked to visitors
and seemed to know what bond she held with them.
The other me remained in milky seas,
amnesia-bound, wrapped in its soft white cloak.

But as I listened to the conscious one
I recognized her story as my own,
and though the conversations slipped away
into the fog, I grasped hold of their key.

Suicide.

Two bottles, held up in a trembling hand
and emptied down my throat in sheer despair,
a final cry to God to pierce the void,
a going off to sleep, wrapped in a rug.

*'Save me, O God, for the waters have come up to my neck. I am sunk in the
miry depths where there is no foothold; I have come into deep waters, swept
and engulfed by the flood. I am weary from calling for help; my throat is
hoarse and parched. My eyes have grown dim from looking for God.' Finally
she found she couldn't read any further for the tears streaming down her
face and the sobs shaking her body. 'Could someone take over, please? I can't
go on . . .' It was all much too close to home and although it was embarrass-
ing to disrupt the communion service like this, there was nothing she could
do to stop the flood.*

So this was where I'd been,
this was the sea:
a cataract of tears
become
a flood.
I had been drowned,
had given up the fight;
having no foothold
I was swept away.
Don't say I didn't struggle,
try to swim—

but in my fear
I drowned myself the more,
until I was so drained,
so limp and faint
I let the waters take me
to my rest.
But this was not to be:
I was washed up
and pulled back
from the depths
to this white bed.

Now I could float,
but only in and out
of consciousness,
of memory,
of life.
How could I tell
these loved-ones
by my bed
my will
was washed away
into despair?

'My brain is an hourglass
from which the sand is draining
draining never to return
seeping
into a well
a vortex
and the walls of my mind
are collapsing

after it
and all that is left
is vacuum
nothingness
insanity.
You can try
to inject life
into this void
but you will fail.
You will fail
as I have failed
miserably
magnificently
and then you must withdraw.
But in a vacuum
where can you
withdraw to?
You can only be crushed
as I am crushed
broken
exhausted.
Oh now do you see my problem?
I can never make myself small enough
but I have to try.'

How could I show them
that I loved them still,
but saw them
through the wrong end
of a telescope?
Suicide
had sucked me

from my feet,
drained me
of my mind,
shrunk me
to a wrung-out self
of shame.
Then it threw me
still screaming
down the cataract,
helpless against
the cruel rocks
below.

*The little girl suddenly realized that she couldn't touch the bottom of the
pool. Fun turned to panic—she screamed out and started to gulp water, to
struggle and flail about. Her big brother was there: she grabbed him round
the neck and hung on to him, pulling him down in the water, too. Although
he could swim and she knew he could save her, the panic continued and her
frantic struggling threatened to drown both of them. He was close, he could
save her, he loved her and wanted to save her, but she was terribly afraid
and couldn't find the trust to relax in his arms.*

She was terribly afraid . . .
She couldn't find the trust . . .
In my fear
I had simply
drowned myself
the more.
Where was the Gardener
then?

'I am with you, always.'
Close. Close.

The Gardener is close,
even when I don't know it.

Pulled from the mire.
Safe. Saved.
The Gardener can save
even a wretch like me.

'See how much I love you—
do you think I'd ever give you up?'
Love. Loved.
The Gardener will love
even when I give Him up as lost.

I was terribly afraid . . .
I couldn't find the trust . . .
yet He preserved my life.

His gentle teaching
soon touched me again,
this time in living form
through my dear dog.
How was I to trust?
By seeing trust,
lavished,
squandered,
poured in love on me.
A spaniel's eyes,
limpid brown pools
of love,
are wells of trust
to quench
the driest thirst.

Everywhere I went
he followed me
or waited for hours
for me to reappear
and then, delighted,
danced for very joy
to see his trust repaid:
'I knew you'd come!'
Rebel by name
but faithful in his deeds,
this little dog
could reach me
once again.

'Be still, my child. Do not fret. Only trust me . . .'
'But I have lost my foothold. I have nowhere to place my feet . . .'

*The girl awoke to the sound of whimpering downstairs. Trixie, the poor old
spaniel, had lost her way again. She was losing the use of her back legs, and
they had to lay down little paths of matting across the parquet floors for her
at night. Even so, she sometimes wandered off the mats and lost her foothold
on the slippery floor. Then she had to wait for one of the family to come down
and lift her back on to the mat. The girl got up and went downstairs: there
was the dog, splayed out in the parquet sea, those trusting, milky, cataract-
filled eyes welcoming her, saying 'I knew you'd save me.' The same trusting
eyes that said 'I know you'll do the best for me' as the vet sent her gently off
to sleep when her suffering was too much. Even after that, the girl still often
woke to what she thought was whimpering in the night and to the thought of
the little helpless animal counting on her, trusting her, waiting for her . . .*

So maybe this was it—
the key to trust.
Be sure,

so sure
of help and love at hand
that asking and receiving
become one,
that giving thanks and waiting
are reversed.
'Whatever you ask for in prayer, believe you have already received it,
   and it shall be yours.'

I pondered this and watched the months go by,
I tried to wait in hope and trust for all.
Recovery became a growing gift,
but would I ever reach the garden now?

I sought its greenness everywhere I went,
but feared the invitation was withdrawn
because I'd sought escape from the true path,
preferred oblivion to the exhausting search.

But then one day in Stanton I was shown
a glimpse, a moment like the earlier ones—
something I could choose to disregard
or cherish as a lesson to be learned.

Sitting
in a muddle
by the stream,
seeing it
fall
and fall again
till it reaches
the garden,
and at first

simply failing
to understand.
Serenity,
the pool
at the heart
of its journey
must be reached
by the falls
or not at all.
It must go
over rocks
and sticks
and mud,
surrender itself
to the torrent
without which
there can be
no peace.
In a way
I had
surrendered myself,
but my surrender
was to fear,
capitulation
to despair,
and that is a torrent
without end.
Now,
as I watched,
a little mossy log
carried a ladybird

safe down the falls
and floated on,
its passenger
intact,
bound for the pool
of peace.
If trust
replaced fear,
if I were
so sure
of love
that fear
could be dissolved,
then I would surrender
my body
to be carried
to the pool,
to the garden
of my dreams.
In my prayer,
as I stopped flailing
and vainly splashing
and relaxed,
I felt a hand
gently supporting
me underneath.
Just a hand,
the same hand
that invited,
courteous
and gentle,

the same hand
that created
the snails,
the hand
that cradled
that poor bird.
Now I could float
not only
in and out
of consciousness—
now I could float
on love.

'Have faith in the Lord your God and you will be upheld.'

Gardener! Gardener! Thank You
for showing me
that Your invitation
is still there.
Thank You
for teaching me
to trust You,
for proving
that,
though I lose hold of You,
You never withdraw Your hand.

THE GARDENER

Be still, my child, and do not fret.
Be still and stop your frantic splashing.
You only need to trust me in your heart,
incline the ear of your heart,

open the eyes of your heart,
and you'll feel my hand there once again.

Turn to me,
gaze on me,
and see how much I love you.
Do you think I'd ever give you up?

Turn to me,
gaze on me,
try to turn away from all your failings.
Do you think I'd banish you for fear?

Turn to me,
gaze on me,
leave me to decide how best to show you
that you,
your struggles,
all your frantic flailing
are for me to gaze on.

You can look at me and find great beauty—
when I gaze on you I find the same.

There is but one entrance to my garden,
down the torrent to the silent pool.
If you try to keep your own firm foothold
you will find the waters fierce and cruel.

All my children try to find their own way
and I always let them choose their path,
but I love them too much to condemn them;
I will not replace my care with wrath.

After you have tried out all the wrong ways
as I know you surely have to do,
my embrace, my gentle invitation,
still remains, a gift to welcome you.

While you fear, your cataracts will blind you
to the only way to get across;
you need only trust me to support you
and you'll see how great gain comes from loss.

Relax. Surrender.
You are a precious jewel to me
and I will carry you
with infinite care
if only you will trust me.

I am the way and the bridge and the door. Enter.

Be still, my child. Do not fret. I am with you, always.

5. A CHAIN OF MOMENTS
Travelling

The fifth paradox: the garden is not just an end for your journey, but the journey itself—while you are travelling, you have it always with you, but do not expect to arrive (*being a lesson in living always in the present moment and being an imperfective verb*)

THE TRAVELLER

And so in trust I persevered and climbed,
hoping to reach the summit and the view,
hoping to find the garden of my dreams
spread out beneath my feet, all wet with dew.

The joy of destination spurred me on
when climbing made me tired and I was sore—
the view I thought was just beyond the ridge
could stretch my vision, coax a few steps more.

That old perfection called me from my past:
another hurdle, just another race—
as though recovery could be achieved,
as though the illness could sink without trace.

So tempting to be perfect once again,
to be made whole, to say goodbye to pain
and not to settle for my mucky self
nor let my body weep or hurt again.

These thoughts were in my mind as I set off
to climb a real hill and to see the view.
The ridge had promised it would open up,
reward my effort as I wished it to.

'I've cracked it.'
That's what I remember thinking.
'I have fought,
I have climbed.
I have won the battle
and recovered.'

Foolish pride.
When I got to the ridge
there was no view, of course,
just another ridge.
I turned
to wander down.

The doctor had teased her about being a perfectionist, saying she could write a better book on the subject than any managed yet. And on the walking holiday he had instructed her to aim for seventy per cent perfection instead. She was blowed if she was going to settle for seventy per cent on this walk, though: all that climbing could only be attempted if the reward of the view from the Devil's Pulpit crowned it all. And it was a magnificent view, only available through this one chink in the wooded hills. On the way down again, she noticed all sorts of little flowers, mosses, tree trunks that had escaped her on the way up, when all she could think of was seventy per cent and how ridiculous it all was, what the view would be like, whether she would get a photo.

But what she really noticed coming down was the process of walking, the chain of moments being put together. And she thought about perfectionism, and about imperfective and perfective verbs in Russian. 'I am walking' would translate one imperfective verb—it is process, a continuous chain of moments. 'I am recovering, I am living, I am experiencing beauty.' The chain of moments—each one an example of the only true perfection, the beauty of God.

50

I turned
to wander down,
dejected,
staring at my feet.
An instant
before crushing it
I saw
there *was* a view.
There glowed
beneath my feet
a six-inch square of earth
scattered with gems
and fragile loveliness.
A brittle leaf,
curled upon itself,
shone gold,
flashed bronze
in a shaft of light.
Was this not a vista
fit for any king,
could I not see here
all that I had sought?

All the time
it lay there,
waiting to be seen,
waiting for my next step
to fall.
I could have crushed it
as I hurried to the ridge.
Fate might have
destroyed it

as I turned.
But no,
although it looked like
a dead leaf
carelessly discarded
by the autumn,
fate was not a player;
the Gardener knew
it still had life
for me.
Here was a six-inch garden,
cradled in the very process
of walking.
Take the next step
and the next
and the next,
consent to weep, and dance, and hurt, and grow.

I had read somewhere
(I think in the Abbé de Tourville)
that perfection
for the Christian
is not like climbing a hill
and seeing a splendid view,
but hunting
in the brambles
and being lost
and scratched,
but knowing it is life
to carry on.
Now that epiphany
came to me,

as the Gardener
showed me how
to travel on.

No, I have not recovered
but the process carries on,
asking of me only
to take the next step.
It hurts, this journey,
and I'm sick of being scratched,
but the garden,
I know,
is in the making of it.
For every now and then
I glimpse its glory;
under a bramble
there are shoots of life;
and I see again
the hand,
that gracious hand,
tending, nurturing, inviting.

Gardener! Gardener!
Thank You for showing me the precious present
for helping me to trust the journey itself.

THE GARDENER

Be still, my child, and do not fret,
be still and rest here in this moment.

You only need to seek me in your heart,
open the eyes of your heart,

incline the ear of your heart
and you will know me with you once again.

Turn to me,
gaze on me
and see how much I love you—
do you think I'd ever leave you now?

Turn to me,
gaze on me,
try to turn away from all your striving—
don't you think I'm journeying with you?

Turn to me,
gaze on me,
leave me to decide how best to show you
that you,
your striving,
all the world's haste
are for me to gaze on.

You can look at me and see great stillness;
when I gaze on you I see the same.

Be still, my child, and do not fret.
My love and grace are for all people.
I am with you, always.

The Garden (II)

Go forward into the day, my soul,
and do not fear,
though the night-time be tormenting
or the morning mournful.
Go forward
with courage and conviction,
carrying your cross
and knowing that Christ has gone before you.
Go forward—
even a single step of faith
will take you further
than any amount of wandering
among worldly cares.
Go forward
though the earth seem to melt away
before you,
for as you place your feet there
the bridge will be built and buttressed
beneath you.
No ifs, no buts, no chasing after shadows—
simply go forward
to where the Master waits to greet you.

Hear the word of the Lord, O nations,
and declare it in the coastlands far away;
say, 'He who scattered the people will gather them . . .
They shall come and sing aloud on the height of Zion
and they shall be radiant over the goodness of the Lord . . .

Their life shall be like a watered garden,
and they shall languish no more.'

'Whoever gives one of these little ones even a cup of cold water because he
is a disciple, truly, I say to you, he will by no means lose his reward . . . As
much as you did it for one of the least of these my children, you did it to me.'

A cup of water—
even a cup of water—
it seems so little,
so insignificant.
What can we change,
whom can we welcome
with so meagre a gift?
Yet this trickle in the desert
could be the difference
between death and life,
could make a plant grow
and blossom, and that could
spread into a tree.
If we all gave a cup of water
we'd have a lake,
and lush vegetation
might sprout up.
Before you knew it
there could be a garden—
a garden with an open gate,
a place of welcome
and an oasis of love.
Just such a garden
is God's gift to us.
But without us

it could die of thirst.
Gracious God—
help us make the garden bloom. *Amen*

Typeset in Garibaldi
by George Tulloch